Carlos Rios-Campos
Gonzalo Orozco Vilema
Oscar Anchundia-Gómez

DIGITAL TRANSFORMATION SUCCESS STORIES

Carlos Rios-Campos
Gonzalo Orozco Vilema
Oscar Anchundia-Gómez

DIGITAL TRANSFORMATION SUCCESS STORIES

ESTONIA AND SINGAPORE

ScienciaScripts

Imprint

Any brand names and product names mentioned in this book are subject to trademark, brand or patent protection and are trademarks or registered trademarks of their respective holders. The use of brand names, product names, common names, trade names, product descriptions etc. even without a particular marking in this work is in no way to be construed to mean that such names may be regarded as unrestricted in respect of trademark and brand protection legislation and could thus be used by anyone.

Cover image: www.ingimage.com

This book is a translation from the original published under ISBN 978-613-9-43306-3.

Publisher:
Sciencia Scripts
is a trademark of
Dodo Books Indian Ocean Ltd. and OmniScriptum S.R.L publishing group

120 High Road, East Finchley, London, N2 9ED, United Kingdom
Str. Armeneasca 28/1, office 1, Chisinau MD-2012, Republic of Moldova, Europe
Printed at: see last page
ISBN: 978-620-8-04628-6

Carlos Rios-Campos

Profession: Doctor in University Management. Master in Administration.

Systems Engineer

. Director of the Institute for Research in Information

and Communication Technology

- IITIC.

Institution: Universidad Nacional Toribio Rodríguez de Mendoza de Amazonas

E-mail: carlos.rios@untrm.edu.pe

Chiclayo, Peru

Gonzalo Orozco Vilema

Profession: Doctor in Educational Sciences, Master in Educational Management,

Specialist in Educational Projects, Urban Architect - Researcher.

Senescyt. Analyst 3 of the Head of Cooperation and Resource Management.

External staff of the Coordination of Internalisation and Academic Mobility, Lecturer

of the Faculty of Philosophy, Letters and Educational Sciences of the Degree

Programme of

Basic Education

Institution: Universidad de Guayaquil

E-mail: ernestoorozcovilema@gmail.com,

gonzalo.orozcov@ug.edu.ec

Guayaquil, Ecuador

Oscar Anchundia-Gómez

Profession: Doctor in Education - Ph.D., Master in University Education and

Educational Research, Bachelor in Computer Science. Former

Director of the Career

Multimedia Systems, Director of the RED-IEB (Red de Docentes Investigadores de

la Carrera Educación Básica) and Docente-Carrera Educación Básica.

Institution: University of Guayaquil - Faculty of Philosophy.

E-mail: oscar.anchundiag@ug.edu.ec

Guayaquil, Ecuador

The educator is the man who makes difficult things look easy.

Ralph Waldo Emerson

Content

1. Introduction 4

2. Digital transformation 6

3. Results 15

4. Conclusions 35

Bibliographical references 37

1. Introduction

The overall objective of this book was to analyse the Digital Transformation Success Stories: Estonia and Singapore.

The coronavirus pandemic has highlighted the need for a strong digital economy to avoid missing the competitiveness train and widening the region's inequality, gender and low productivity gaps (United Nations, 2020).

Digital technology will be the key driver of change in this century, reshaping economies, governments and civil society, and impacting every aspect of our work, sometimes in unexpected ways. With this in mind, UNDP launched its first organisation-wide digital strategy in 2019 (Opp, 2021).

The good news is that digital transformation can help LAC economies emerge from the crisis by stimulating business innovation and new consumption patterns, transforming production systems and value chains, reorganising economic sectors and introducing new conditions for competitiveness (ECLAC, 2020).

According to BBVA Research, some countries have achieved levels of digitisation above those expected based on their income levels. This is

the case of Singapore, Korea, Japan, the United States, the United
Kingdom and the countries of northern and central Europe (Cabirta, 2019).

2. Digital transformation

Digital transformation is what happens when companies adopt new and innovative ways of doing business based on technological advances. It is the process of changing something completely with digital tools (Red Hat, 2021).

Digital transformation is generally recognised by the analysis sample as being of vital importance for organisational success (Cuenca-Fontbona, Matilla & Compte-Pujol, 2020).

Digital transformation in organisations is possible, necessary and critical to start as soon as possible and will be feasible if the teams that have to implement it know in detail the vision and strategy of the organisation...(Juca, Brito, B., García & Burgo, 2019).

Figure 1. Digital transformation in organisations.

Source: https://secatel.com/que-es-la-transformacion-digital

The current process of digital transformation and the enormous strategic benefits and forecasts achieved in areas of activity such as industry and retail have generated different theoretical and practical proposals for its implementation and development in non-economic areas such as politics, education, healthcare and, more worryingly, morality (Calvo, 2019).

It is, in general, the way we work, learn and live that make technology a crucial force for economic competitiveness and social development (Anzola, 2019).

The result is a real social transformation: ICTs are changing the way we relate to each other, work or fill our leisure space (Muñoz, Díaz & Gallego, 2020).

On the other hand, new digital technologies, education-oriented Internet resources and approaches concerning the reduction of the digital divide in the educational context are highlighted (Vargas-Murillo, 2020).

There is an objective relationship between the level of sophistication of national innovation systems and the quality of digitisation of university management functions (Dudin, Afanasyev, Voropaev & Zasko, 2020).

The conclusion reached is that digitisation should be seen as an opportunity to improve governance, through the restructuring of public services, intensively using digital technologies in order to increase their effectiveness and efficiency to achieve the digital well-being of citizens and substantial savings (Huamán & Medina, 2022).

Figure 2. Digital transformation in public administration.

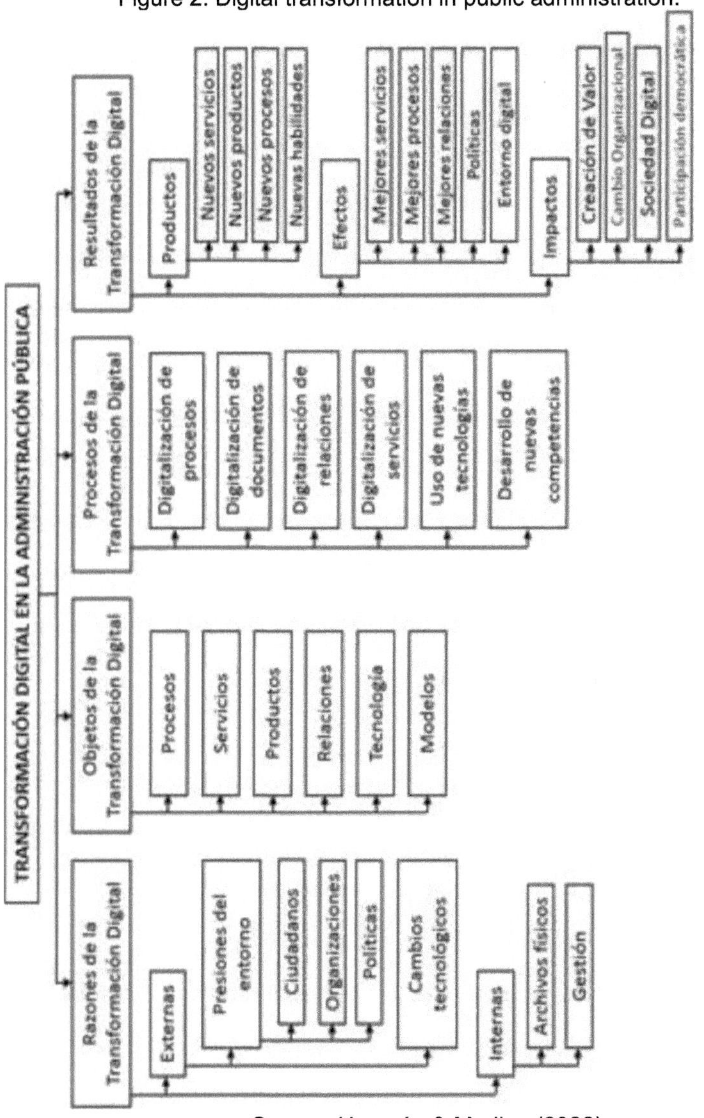

Source: Huamán & Medina (2022)

9

Another area of dynamic interest is information studies in e-government and e-democracy, as well as in smart cities or in digital learning and inclusion (Paletta and Moreiro-Gonzalez, 2021).

It is possible to affirm that the influence and adoption of digital government in different countries contributes to bringing citizens and the state closer together, increasing transparency and improving services.... In short, digital government allows access to information in a flexible and reliable way. In this way, government can provide inclusiveness, reliability in service delivery and improve the quality of life of citizens (Pérez, 2020).

Among the main challenges are planning, the adaptation of methodologies and curricula, the change of mentality, and how to achieve through digital transformation an efficient integration and management of all those involved in an organisation...(Ospina, & Navarrete, 2020).

And this strategic need requires a strong willingness to address, from the inside, the needs of change: from technology to people. Because any digital transformation, in order to be successful, must focus on three issues: technology, processes and people (Benítez, 2020).

Finally, the continuing sense that digital transformation is occurring at a (much) slower pace than expected is related to multiple factors, not least of which is the fear that digital transformers will eventually be replaced by the technology itself (Vacas, 2018).

The digital transformation is a fact, Guedes pointed out, and data, which is constantly growing, is the official and most valuable currency of this revolution. Blockchain, machine learning and big data are the answers to this incessant production of knowledge that requires order, regulatory framework, evolution and solutions (Elsevier Connect, 2018).

The blockchain application is a technological innovation that promises to revolutionise the way commodities in the oil sector are traded, through the use of cryptographic techniques that allow the streamlining of complex transactions that are being applied in trade and business (Sanchez, 2020).

Figure 3. How the blockchain works

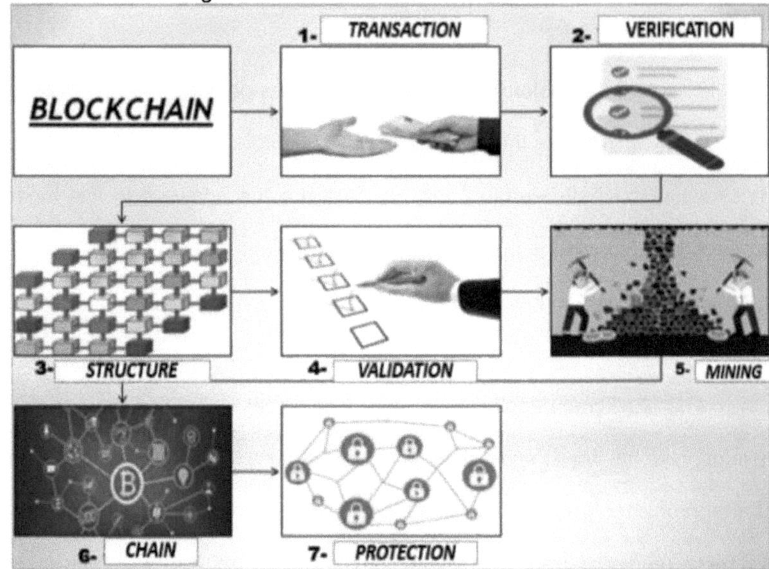

Source: Sanchez (2020)

This means that digital transformation is seen not as a simple implementation of new technologies but as "digital education", since once we are able to understand how they work we will also be able to apply them (Alayón, 2021).

Figure 4. The 4 axes of digital transformation

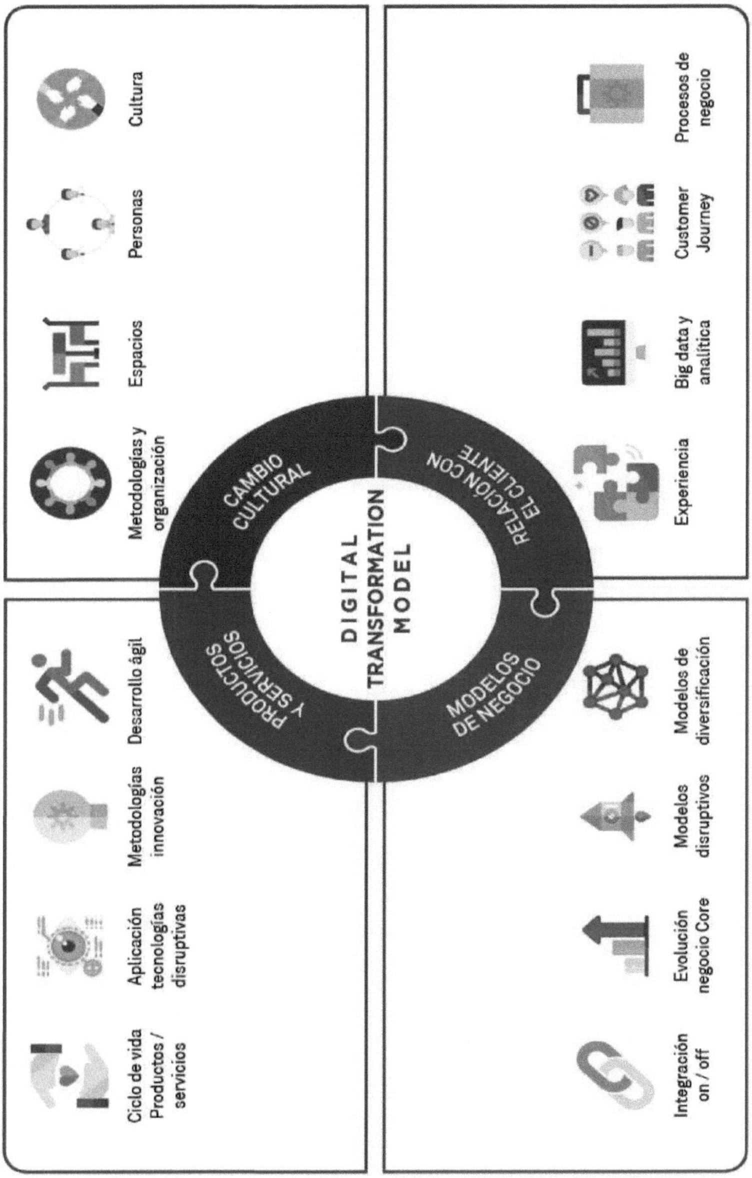

Source: The Valley Digital Business School (2021).

Figure 4 shows the 4 axes of digital transformation, which are products and services, cultural change, business models and customer relations.

Digital masters cultivate two capabilities: digital capability, which enables them to use innovative technologies to improve elements of their business, and leadership capability, which enables them to envision and drive organisational change in a systematic and cost-effective way. Together, these two capabilities enable a firm to transform digital technology into a competitive advantage (Bonnet & Westerman, 2021).

Currently, 244 million Latin Americans - 38% of the population - do not have access to the Internet, a social gap that deepens inequality in terms of access to knowledge and opportunities. This gap is accentuated within the countries of the region, between urban and rural populations, as well as between men and women, and between young people and older adults (CAF, 2020).

Digital transformation is important and urgent for organisations and countries, especially in these times of pandemic. Therefore, efforts must be made to implement it, especially in Latin America, where the digital divide is widening.

3. Results

Fortunately, effective practices to transform government, services, communities, cities and businesses are emerging in countries at the forefront. Among the most efficient approaches are: taking a holistic view of ICT and complementary investments; mobilising demand for good governance and better services; and promoting public-private partnerships, among others (Hanna, 2017).

Figure 5. Countries ranked according to the 2021 Internet Inclusion Index.

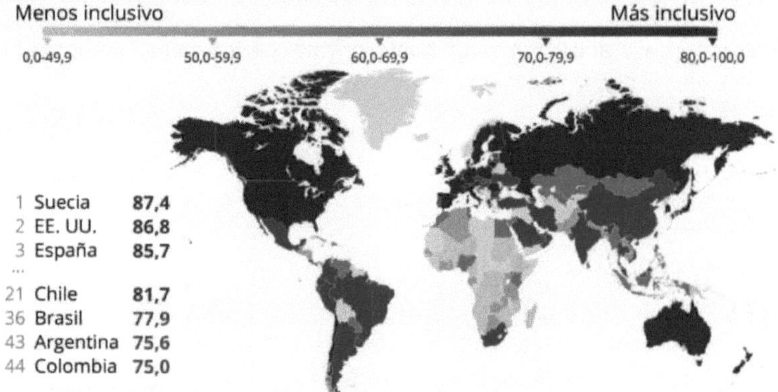

Source: Statista (2021)

Figure 5 shows that Sweden is the most inclusive country in Internet 2021, thanks to ongoing investment and appropriate state policy.

The International Telecommunication Union (ITU), together with the Ministry of Foreign Affairs of the Republic of Estonia (MRE Estonia), the Federal Ministry for Economic Cooperation and Development of the Federal Republic of Germany (BMZ) and the Digital Impact Alliance (DIAL) of the United Nations Foundation, have signed a joint declaration to accelerate digital transformation and digitisation of government services, especially in low-resource settings (ITU, 2020).

The digital transformation process in the Estonian and Singaporean cases is described below.

3.1. The case of Estonia

The capital of Estonia is Tallinn, **Official languages of the EU**: Estonian, **EU Member State**: since 1 May 2004, **Currency**: euro... .Estonia is a parliamentary republic. Its head of government - the prime minister - is appointed by the president and approved by the parliament. He is responsible for the executive power vested in the government. The head of state - the president - is elected by the parliament or electoral college for a five-year term. The 101-member Parliament is elected by direct suffrage every 4 years. The country is divided into 15 provinces and 79 municipalities (European Union, 2021).

Estonia is one of the three Baltic countries that are among the most advanced nations in the teaching and use of information and communication technologies. In 1991, after gaining independence from the Soviet Union, Estonia opted to promote the digital economy and mass technological innovation, due to the fact that it was a tiny country lacking its own natural resources (Roonemaa, 2017).

This small country was born with no money, no technology and no institutions. It had to start from scratch and therefore relied on human talent specialised in numbers and cryptography (Semana, 2020).

The new nation's first passports were issued in 1992, and when, a decade later, it was time for renewal, the government went one step further and provided the identity card with an electronic chip to access its online services. Today, 99 per cent of official procedures - a total of 1,789... (Collera, 2018).

About 25 years ago, the Estonian public sector set itself the goal of developing e-government and the government started to develop databases, to enhance a secure environment for information exchange and digital certification, and to promote the creation of e-services (Holm, 2020).

In 2000, this small Baltic state became the first country to pass a Telecommunications Act declaring internet access a universal right. In the same year, the Council of Ministers abolished paper and citizens were allowed to file their tax returns online (Cerdeira, 2020).

Estonia is one of the most advanced countries in the world in digital transformation, where 99% of public and private procedures are done online; the mobile phone acts as an identity document, a means of payment and a tool for signing any document; and where the time it takes to set up a business is three hours (Confiep, 2019).

Table 1. International cyber incidents (2003-2020)

Año	Incidente
2003	Acusación de EEUU a China sobre ataques informáticos (Titan Rain).
2007	Ataques a Estonia que inutilizaron infraestructuras críticas.
2008	Explosión, por ataque cibernético, del oleoducto BTC en Refahiye (Turquía).
2010	El gusano informático *Stuxnet* genera daños en plantas de uranio iraníes y sabotea proyectos estratégicos nacionales.
2012	Borrado de 30.000 discos duros de la empresa petrolera Saudí Aramco.
2016	Presunto ciberataque ruso (servicios de seguridad rusos) en las elecciones presidenciales de EEUU con filtraciones de información de los servidores de correo del Comité Nacional Demócrata y de su candidata Hillary Clinton, publicación de documentos para afectar su imagen y posible manipulación de elecciones en favor de Donald Trump.
2018	Supuestos ciberataques contra estructuras de información de Rusia en la copa mundial de futbol y contra redes de suministro eléctrico en 2019.
2019	Presuntos ataques cibernéticos a la infraestructura eléctrica de Venezuela.
2020	Acusaciones entre potencias por presuntos ataques cibernéticos para robo de propiedad intelectual e información sobre vacunas COVID 19.
2020	Intrusión a la plataforma de videoconferencias Zoom para extraer información, infiltrar datos y boicotear reuniones remotas.

Source: Ospina & Sanabria (2020).

Table 1 shows the cyber incident that occurred in 2007, when Estonia suffered a major cyber attack in which its critical infrastructure was disabled.

This system is based on x-road, a secure open source data exchange platform, which allows access to 3000 different procedures / services. Data protection is ensured through the use of blockchain technology. Estonians trust and use online solutions because they are fast, secure and convenient (Accessr, 2020).

Figure 6. The local-national-international scale of the Soldier of the Year crisis.

Bronze and the Tallinn 2007 cyber-attacks

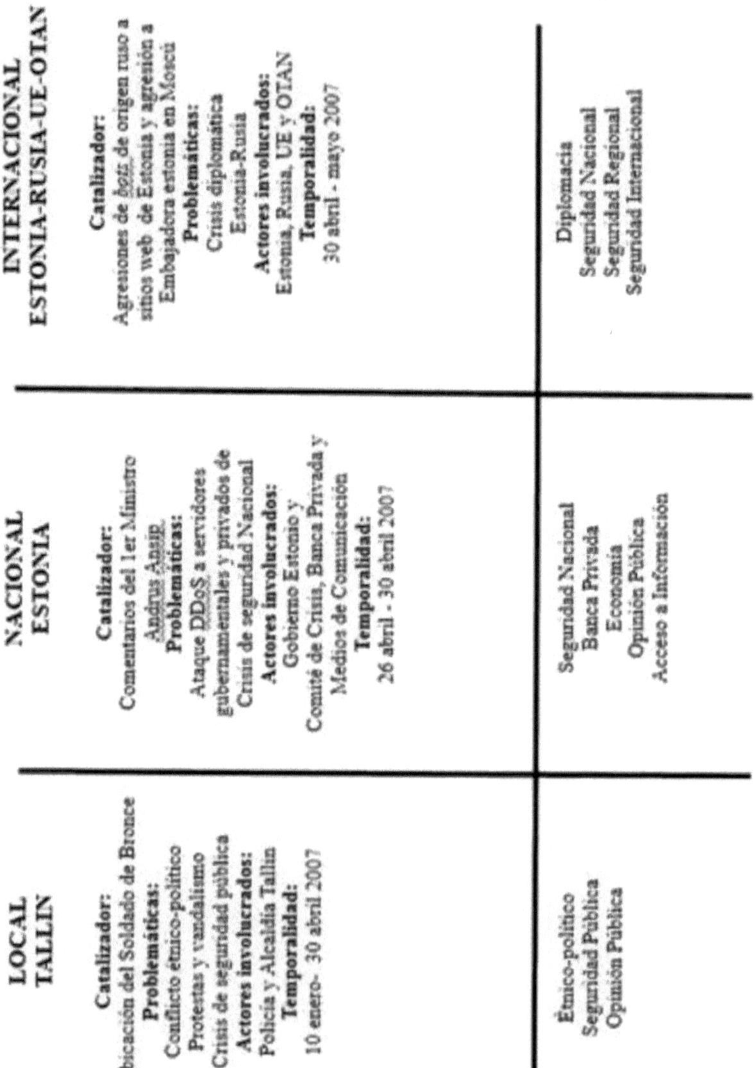

Source: Aguilar (2019)

Figure 6 shows the escalation of the crisis that culminated in the cyber attacks on Estonia during the period 30 April to May 2007.

According to MICITT (2019), thanks to the support and liaison provided by the Inter-American Development Bank to bring Costa Rica closer to the Estonian digital government experience, several agreements were signed in which work will be carried out on:
1. Knowledge exchange for the development of effective digital economy and governance solutions.
2. Development of a roadmap and implementation of relevant platforms for data exchange and connection of institutions.
3. Promotion and cooperation between technology companies and communities for the development of digital services between the two countries.
4. Digital Identity Development.
5. Training and exchange of experiences in cybersecurity and critical infrastructure protection.
6. Promotion of cooperation between educational institutions.

Estonia managed to contain the epidemic. The article argues that crisis management was facilitated by political factors, rapid policy learning, cooperation with the scientific community, and the infrastructure of information and communication technologies and digital governance (Raudla, 2021).

Figure 7. Website for obtaining Estonian e-residency.

Source: E-resident (2021)

Figure 7 shows the website of Estonia, which is the first country to offer e-

Residency, a government-issued digital identity and status that provides access to Estonia's transparent business environment: a new digital nation for the world. Internet-resident entrepreneurs from all over the world can start an EU-based company and manage their business from anywhere, completely online (E-resident, 2021).

e-Residency is available for citizens from all over the world. You can start the procedure from this website.

Estonia's economy is innovative and knowledge-based, using new technologies and business models and flexible forms of employment. Favourable conditions have been created for R&D and innovation in the private sector, and researchers and companies are cooperating. Estonia's business environment attracts people to work here, start companies or engage in virtual business, invest and create and test new solutions that benefit society at large (Valitsus, 2021).

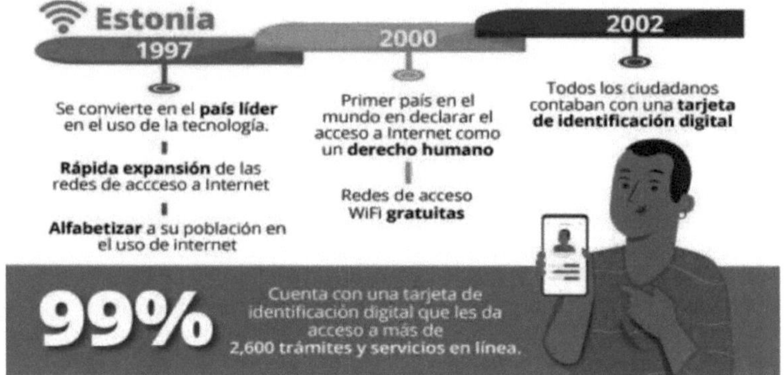

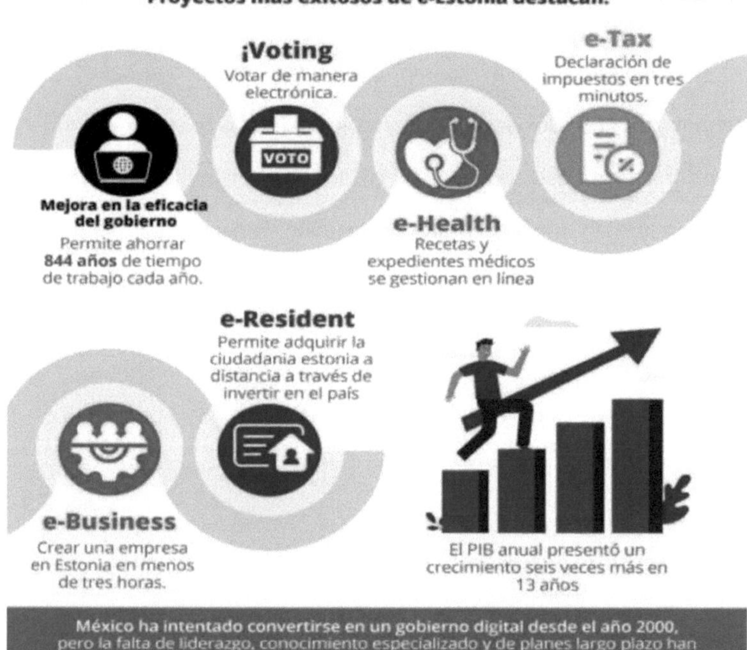

Source: Marcopaz (2021)

Figure 8 shows Estonia, as a successful digital government, whose most prominent projects are: Improving government efficiency e-voting, e-health, e-filing of taxes, e-business and e-residency.

As a highly digitised country, it is highly exposed to cyber-attacks, which is why Estonia is making continuous efforts to avoid a crisis similar to the one in 2007.

3.2. Singapore case

Singapore is made up of 64 islands including the main island known as Singapore Island or Pulau Ujong. This island is linked to the Malaysian mainland by two bridges. The first leads to the border town of Johor Bahru in Malaysia. The second, further west, also connects to Johor Bahru in the neighbourhoods of the Tuas region (Outer, 2021).

In 1959, when Singapore had just been granted self-rule by the UK, Lee Kuan Yew was elected Prime Minister. In 1963, Singapore joined the Federation of Malaysia. However, disagreements between the federal and local governments led to final Singaporean independence on 9 August 1965 with Lee Kuan Yew at the helm of the 2 million Singaporeans who were the result of Chinese, Indian and Malay immigrants (Mandujano, 2021).

Source: Foreign Affairs (2021)

Figure 9 shows the map of Singapore, which shows the large number of islands that make up its territory.

The fourth richest nation on the planet, in terms of the per capita purchasing power of its inhabitants, is no bigger than the so-called capital of the world, New York. A member of the select club of city-states, along with the Vatican and Monaco, Singapore has just 5.7 million inhabitants...(Bonet, 2021).

Singapore ranked first with strong performance in all seven components (Basic Needs, Government and Business Investment, Ease of Doing Business, Human Capital, Start-up Environment, Technology Adoption and Technology Infrastructure), including the highest score in Human Capital and Business and Government Investment (Cisco, 2020).

A change of mindset was needed, said Minister Zulkifli. "Our approach has been to build a liveable and sustainable city, through pragmatic policy based on sound economic and scientific principles; a focus on long-term planning and effective implementation; and the ability to mobilise popular support for the common good" (UNEP, 2018).

We understand that people are our only resource, so if we need to develop anything it is to develop people. That's why our strong investment in education and focus, I think it's not just from the government, it's a cultural norm for Asians to invest in education. In general that's how Chinese culture is, and Singapore is 75% Chinese (TEC Observatory, 2020).

The system has been incorporated into the national digital identity card - known as *SingPass* (Singapore Personal Access) - which since 2003 has enabled some 3.3 million Singapore citizens, just over half of the total population, to connect to more than 400 public and private services (Almoguera, 2020).

Singapore is all about technology. Its residents already have fibre optic networks stretching the length and breadth of the island, providing them with high-speed internet, and there are already three mobile phones for every two citizens (BBC World, 2017).

Progress continues to be made in the citizen-centric approach as it evolves according to the changing preferences of citizens. With the establishment of excellent internet infrastructure and the online availability of government data, e-participation is expected to grow as it begins to form an integral part of government service delivery and interaction with the public (Pantzer, 2016).

Figure 10. Singapore's Go Digital Programme.

Source: IMDA (2021).

Figure 10 shows Singapore's Go Digital Programme from the Infocomm Media Development Authority (IMDA), which has 3 steps: Is your digital business ready, how did you get started and where can you get help?

Singapore's innovation model is based on the influence of the public sector over the private sector. The government first identifies those sectors that are strategic for the country and those in which it has the capacity to influence. Once identified, it announces its intention to invest and invest heavily in these sectors and contacts large companies in the sector to establish public-private partnerships with both universities and public agencies (Sánchez, 2021).

The fintech sector is already a consolidated market in Singapore, with a wide range of accelerators, open innovation programmes with the country's main financial institutions, including the three local banks DBS, OCBC and UOB, as well as a large number of international banks based in the commercial hub that Singapore represents in Southeast Asia, and significant institutional support (Sanchez, 2020).

Table 2. The fintech sector in Singapore.

Datum	Figure	Change previous year	Source
Total *fintech* investment Singapore (2019)	+1 billion SGD	+12 %	Monetary Authority of Singapore (MAS)
Number of *fintech startups* (2019)	+1.100	-	MORE
Global Fintech Ranking (2019)	3.°	[18	Findexable
IFZ Global FinTech Ranking (2018)	1°	-	Thomson Reuters Labs
Companies in the Fintech100 (2019)	4	-	KPMG
Financial sector as a percentage of GDP (2019)	13,9%	+0,7 %	Singstat
The Global Financial Centres Index	5°	-1	Z/Yen Group
No. of banking licences	204	-	MORE
No. of insurance licences	351	-	MORE
Nº licences means of payment	466		MORE

Source: Sanchez (2020).
Table 2 shows the increase in total investment in fintechs.

of Singapore, according to the Monetary Authority of Singapore (MAS).

The Singapore FinTech Festival, organised by the Monetary Authority of Singapore, the Singapore FinTech Festival (SFF) is in its sixth year. Last year's annual event brought together 60,000 participants from 160 countries, both virtually and in person, for financial services, public policy and technology development (Singapore Fintech Festival, 2021).

Figure 11. Singapore Fintech Festival website.

Source: Singapore Fintech Festival (2021)

Figure 11 shows the Singapore Fintech Festival website, which offers access to sponsors and exhibitors, agenda, community, about, certification and registration.

In Estonia and Singapore, the strong investment by the state and the commitment and adaptation of their society to the changes of digital transformation stand out.

4. Conclusions

The 4 axes of digital transformation are products and services, cultural change, business models and customer relations.

Digital transformation is important and urgent for organisations and countries, especially in these times of pandemic. Therefore, efforts must be made to implement it, especially in Latin America, where the digital divide is widening.

Sweden is the most inclusive country in Internet 2021, thanks to continued investment and appropriate state policy.

In the 2007 Estonian cyber incident, Estonia's critical infrastructure was crippled and the crisis escalated during the period from 30 April to May 2007.

The Estonian website offers e-Residency, a government-issued digital identity and status that provides access to Estonia's transparent business environment: a new digital nation for the world.

Estonia is a successful digital government, whose most prominent projects are: Improved government efficiency, e-voting, e-health, e-filing, e-business and e-residency.

The Infocomm Media Development Authority's (IMDA) Go Digital

Singapore Programme, which has 3 steps: Is your business digital ready, how did you get started and where can you get help?

There is evidence of an increase in total investment in fintech in Singapore, according to the Monetary Authority of Singapore (MAS).

The Singapore Fintech Festival website offers access to sponsors and exhibitors, agenda, community, about, certification and registration.

Estonia and Singapore are two success stories of digital transformation, which is why many countries seek their advice and establish agreements. This digital transformation process has required constant effort and a high level of commitment from the actors involved.

Bibliographical references

Accessr (2020). E-stonia, the most connected country in the world.

Retrieved from https://accessr.eu/en/projets/e-stonia-the-

most-

connected-country-in-the-world/

Aguilar, Juan Antonio Manuel (2019). Cyber-physical facts: an analysis proposal for cyberthreats in National Cybersecurity Strategies. URVIO Latin American Journal of Security Studies, (25), 24-40. https://doi.org/10.17141/urvio.25.2019.4007

Alayón Rodríguez, E. E. (2021). Disruptive technologies in the digital transformation of organisations in Industry 4.0. Scientific Magazine, 6(21), 267-281. https://doi.org/10.29394/Scientific.issn.2542- 2987.2021.6.21.14.267-281

Almoguera, P. (2020). Singapore debuts face verification system as ID card

.   retrieved   from

https://elpais.com/retina/2020/10/02/innovacion/1601653052_245522.ht ml

Anzola Montero, G. (2019). Digital transformation for the industrial revolution: the new call for the U.D.C.A. Rev. U.D.C.A Act. & Div. Cient. 22(1):e1228. https://doi.org/10.31910/rudca.v22.n1.2019.1228 Barrero, A. and Rosero, A. (2018). Estado del Arte sobre Concepciones de la Diversidad en el Contexto

Escolar Infantil. Latin American Journal of Inclusive Education, 2018, 12(1), 39-55 https://doi.org/10.4067/S0718- 73782018000100004

BBC World (2017). Singapore: what the world's most expensive country is doing to become the smartest. Retrieved from https://www.bbc.com/mundo/noticias-38894741

Benítez, E. (2020). The digital transformation of the external control of public spending. Auditoría Pública n° 76,   pp.19 - 30. https://asocex.es/wp-content/uploads/2020/11/Revista-Auditoria-Publica-n%C2%BA-76-pag-   19-a-30.pdf

Bonet, I. (2021). Singapore, the Asian Monaco of the mega-rich. Retrieved from
                   https://elpais.com/gente/2021-09-14/singapur-la-monaco-asiatic-megarricos.html

Bonnet, D. & Westerman, G. (2021). The new elements of digital transformation. Business Review (No. 308) - ICT - February.
Retrieved from https://www.harvard-deusto.com/los-nuevos-elementos-de-la-transformacion-digital

CAF (2020). Digital transformation for 21st century Latin America.   Retrieved from https://www.caf.com/es/conocimiento/visiones/2020/02/transformacion- digital-for-the-latin-america-of-s21/

Cabirta, A. (2019). Which are the most digitised countries? Retrieved from https://www.bbva.com/es/cuales-son-los-paises-mas- digitised/

Calvo, Patrici (2019). Etification, La transformación digital de lo moral* * This study is part of the Scientific Research and Technological Development Project FFI2016-76753-c2-2-p, funded by the Ministry of Economy and Competitiveness, and uji-a2016-04, funded by the Universitat Jaume I. Kriterion: Revista de Filosofia, v. 60, n. 144, pp. 671-688. Available at: <https://doi.org/10.1590/0100-512X2019n14409pc>.

ECLAC (2020). Latin America and the Caribbean: digital transformation is key to accelerating recovery and ensuring better reconstruction, says new report. Retrieved from https://www.cepal.org/es/comunicados/america-latina-caribe-la-transformacion-digital-es-clave-acelerar-la-recuperacion

Cerdeira, L. (2020). What we can learn from Estonia, the most   digitised country in the world .

https://forbes.es/empresas/76138/lo-que-podemos-aprender-de-estonia- el-pais-mas-digitalizados-del-mundo/

Cisco (2020). Cisco study reveals how ready countries are to create a digital economy in which all citizens can participate and thrive. Retrieved from https://news- blogs.cisco.com/americas/en/2020/03/11/cisco-study-reveals-countries'-readiness-to-build-a-digital-economy-in-which-all-citizens-can-participate-and-thrive/

Collera, V. (2018). Estonia, the world's first digital country. Retrieved from https://elpais.com/elpais/2018/04/05/eps/1522927807_984041 .html

Confiep (2019). Digital transformation and innovation in companies: the Estonian case. retrieved from https://www.confiep.org.pe/noticias/actualidad/transformacion-digital-e-innovation-in-companies-the-case-of-estonia/

Cuenca-Fontbona, Joan, Matilla, Kathy, & Compte-Pujol, Marc (2020). Digital transformation of public relations and communication departments in a sample of Spanish companies. Revista de Comunicación, 19(1), 75-92. https://dx.doi.org/10.26441/rc19.1-2020-a5

Dudin, M., Afanasyev, V., Voropaev, M. & Zasko, V. (2020). Status and problems of digitization of university management in Russia and three Latin American countries (Argentina, Chile and Brazil). Form. Univ. vol. 13n. 6. http://dx.doi.org/

Elsevier Connect (2018). Digital transformation of the health sector: situation map and trends. Retrieved from https://www.elsevier.com/es-en/connect/ehealth/transformacion-digital-del-sector-salud-mapa-de- situacion-y-tendencias

E-resident (2021). The new digital nation. Retrieved from https://www.e-resident.gov.ee/

Foreign Affairs (2021). Singapore - Ministry of Foreign Affairs. Retrieved from

http://www.exteriores.gob.es/documents/fichaspais/singapur_ficha%20p ais.pdf

Hanna, N. (2017) How can developing countries make the most of the digital revolution? Retrieved from https://blogs.worldbank.org/es/voices/como-pueden-los-paises-en-development-maximising-the-digital-revolution.

Holm, J. (2020). Digital transformation in the Estonian public sector Benefits and challenges for the National Audit Office. Revista española de control externo, Vol. 22, No. Extra 64, pp. 22-47. Retrieved from https://dialnet.unirioja.es/descarga/articulo/7768609.pdf

Huamán Coronel, Pepe Luis, & Medina Sotelo, Cristian Gumercindo (2022). Digital transformation in public administration: challenges for active governance in Peru. Comuni@cción, 13(2), 93-105. https://dx.doi.org/10.33595/2226-1478.13.2.594

IMDA (2021). SMEs GoDigital . retrievedfrom https://www.imda.gov.sg/programme-listing/smes-go-digital

Juca Maldonado, F., Brito, B., García Saltos, M. B., & Burgo Bencomo, O. B. (2019). Digital transformation in university academic processes as an alternative to reduce the impact on the environment. Revista Conrado, 15(67), 309-316. Retrieved from http://conrado.ucf.edu.cu/index.php/conrado

Mandujano, J. (2021). Singapore's economic advancement: Independence and the beginnings of the island nation . Retrieved from http://pueaa.unam. mx/blog/avance-econom ico-de-singapore-primera- parte.

Marcopaz (2021). E-Estonia, a successful digital government. Retrieved from http://marcopaz.mx/2021/05/20/e-estonia-un-gobierno-digital-exitoso/

MICITT (2019). Costa Rica and Estonia sign cooperation agreements on Digital

Government and The Fourth Industrial Revolution. Retrieved from

https://www.micitt.go.cr/portaldos/index.php?option=com_content&view=

article&id=10535:teletrabajo-es-ley-de-la- republica&catid=40&Itemid=1917

Muñoz, L., Díaz, E. & Gallego, S. (2020). The responsibilities derived from the

use of information and communication technologies in the practice of health

professions. Anales de Pediatría, Volume 92, Issue 5,Pages307.   5,

Pages307.e1-307.e6.

https://doi.org/10.1016/j.anpedi.2020.03.003.

United Nations (2020). The digital divide must not become a new face of

inequality in Latin America. Retrieved from

https://news.un.org/es/story/2020/09/1481182

TEC Observatory (2020). Learn about Singapore's successful education model.

retrieved   from   https://observatorio.tec.mx/edu-

news/interview-mike-thiruman-general-secretary-teachers-union-singapore

Opp, R. (2021). Digital technology is transforming development. UNDP is

also   Transforming too.   retrieved   from

https://www1.undp.org/content/undp/es/home/blog/2021/digital-is-   changing-

development--undp-is-changing-too--.html

Ospina Díaz, Milton Ricardo, & Sanabria Rangel, Pedro Emilio (2020). Desafíos nacionales frente a la ciberseguridad en el escenario global: un análisis para Colombia. Revista Criminalidad, 62(2), 199-217. Epub November26 , 2020. Retrievedfrom http://www.scielo.org.co/scielo.php?script=sci_arttext&pid=S1794-31082020000200199&lng=en&tlng=es.

Ospina Usaquén, M. Ángel, & Navarrete Cárdenas, L. C. (2020). Characterization of the main challenges of the implementation of digital transformation in engineering education in Colombia. Encuentro Internacional De Educación En Ingeniería. Retrieved from https://acofipapers.org/index.php/eiei/article/view/772

Paletta, F. C. and Moreiro-González, J. A. (2021). The digital transformation in the methods and topics of Brazilian Information and Documentation research 2010-2019. Revista Española de Documentación Científica, 44 (2), e293. https://doi.org/ 10.3989/redc.2021.2.1763

Pantzer, R. (2016). Singapore and its cutting-edge technology. Retrieved from https://blogs.iadb.org/administracion-publica/es/singapur-y-su-cutting-edge-technology/

Pérez, Baena, F. A. (2020). Digital government strategy for building more transparent and proactive states. Trilogía Ciencia TecnologíaSociedad , 12(22), 71-102. https://doi.org/10.22430/21457778.1235

Raudla, Ringa (2021). Estonia's response to the COVID-19 pandemic: learning, cooperation and the advantages of being a small country. Revista de Administração Pública, v. 55, n. 1. https://doi.org/10.1590/0034-761220200414.

Red Hat (2021). Digital transformation: What is digital transformation? Retrieved from https://www.redhat.com/es/topics/digital- transformation/what-is-digital-transformation

Roonemaa, M. (2017). The Baltic 'digital tiger'. Retrieved from https://es.unesco.org/courier/abril-junio-2017/tigre-digital-baltico

Sánchez, C. (2020). Sector factsheet. The fintech market in Singapore 2020. Retrieved from https://www.icex. en/icex/en/navegacion-principal/all-our-services/market-information/countries/navegacion-principal/el-mercado/estudios- informes/DOC2020857012.html?idPais=SG

Sánchez, F. (2021). The innovation and entrepreneurship model in Singapore.

Boletín económico de ICE, Información Comercial Española, N° 3132 (From 1 to 28 FEBRUARY 2021), pp. 61-71. https:/doi.org/10.32796/bice.2021.3132.7152

Sánchez Cano, Julieta Evangelina (2020). The technological innovation of the blockchain and its impact on the energy sector. Panorama económico (Mexico City), 16(31), 157-178. Epub 23 February 2021.https://doi.org/10.29201/pe-ipn.v16i31.267

Statista (2021). Countries ranked according to The Economist Intelligence Unit's Internet Inclusion Index 2021. Retrieved from https://es.statista.com/grafico/25716/paises-y-territorios-clasificados- segun-el-indice-de-inclusion-de-internet/

Week (2020). The incredible story of Estonia, the most digital country in the world. Retrieved from https://www.semana.com/economia/articulo/la- unbelievable-history-of-estonia-the-most-digital-country-in-the-world/202011/

Singapore Fintech Festival (2021). About Us. Retrieved from https://www.fintechfestival.sg/about-us/

The Valley Digital Business School (2021). Digital Transformation Model.

Retrieved from https://thevalley.es/scale/

ITU (2020). ITU, Estonia, Germany and DIAL join forces to accelerate the digital transformation of government services. Retrieved from https://www.itu.int/es/mediacentre/Pages/cm06-2020-   ITU-Estonia-Germany-DIAL-digital-transformation-government.aspx

UNEP (2018). Singapore's journey to become a biodiversity role model. Retrieved from https://www.unep.org/es/noticias-y-   reports/reports/the-singapore-journey-to-become-a-model-of

Union   European Union   (2021).   Estonia.
            retrievedfrom
https://europa.eu/european-union/about-eu/countries/member-
countries/estonia_en
Vacas, F. (2018). Digital transformation: from facelift to reconversion.
CEF, No. 10 (May-August 2018), pp. 135-143). Retrieved from
https://dialnet.unirioja.es/descarga/articulo/6775335.pdf

Valitsus   (2021).   Strategic   goals.   retrievedfrom
https://www.valitsus.ee/en/estonia-2035-development-
stategy/strategy/strategic-goals

Vargas-Murillo, G. (2020). Educational strategies and digital technology in the teaching-learning process. Cuadernos Hospital de Clínicas, 61(1), 114-129. Recovered from http://www.scielo.org.bo/scielo.php?script=sci_arttext&pid=S1652-67762020000100010&lng=es&tlng=es.

Printed by Books on Demand GmbH, Norderstedt / Germany